Losing an Empire, Finding a Role